ABIDING STORIES

ABIDING STORIES

Compiled by
MICHAEL WELLS

Illustrated by
Bob Fuller

Abiding Life Press

© 2005 by Michael Wells

Published by Abiding Life Press
A division of Abiding Life Ministries International
P.O. Box 620998, Littleton, CO 80162

Printed in the United States of America

All rights reserved. No part of this publication may be reproduced, stored in a retrieval system, or transmitted in any form or by any means—electronic, mechanical, photocopy, recording, or any other—without the prior written permission of the publisher. The only exception is brief quotations in printed reviews.

Library of Congress Cataloging-in-Publication Data		
Wells, Michael, 1952-		
Abiding Stories/Michael Wells		
p. cm.		
ISBN 0-9670843-3-4		
1. Christian Life—1960—2. Presence of God. I. Title.		
BV4501.2.W41818	1993	93-31241
BV4501.2.W4182	1991	90-49987 CIP
248.4—dc20		

Scripture quotations are from the New American Standard Bible, © the Lockman Foundation 1960, 1962, 1963, 1968, 1971, 1972, 1973, 1975, 1977 or are from the New International Version, copyright 1985 by The Zondervan Corporation.

To the God of the greatest story ever told.

ACKNOWLEDGMENTS

This book would never have been printed without help from the following people:

Bob Fuller, Fuller Creative, who turns imaginations into images that illustrate and embellish this entire book, cover to cover.

Dawn Paul, Dawn Paul Design, whose creativity is revealed in every page.

Betty Wells, my editor, to whom I have proven I have yet to run out of something to say.

All the storytellers, from near and far, who entertain and enlighten our world.

Contents

1	Introduction
3	The Stressed Vine
5	Red-Faced Monkey
9	Worms For Feathers
11	The Richest Man in the City
13	The Precious One Minute
15	The Boxing Ring
19	The Lost Key
21	The Little Fish
23	Rats!
25	Money Isn't Everything
29	You Can't Put Water in a Full Cup!
31	The Perfect Photo
35	The Mysterious String
37	The Great Meal in Heaven!
39	The Man in the Balcony
41	Your True Nature
43	Being Content
45	The Cracked Pot
49	Where to Find the Light?
53	A Perfect Power
55	Little Girl
57	How to Be Acceptable
59	Goat Priest
61	The Mogul King
63	Choose the Easy Way Today and Prepare for the Harder Way Later!
65	The Vine and the Branch
67	God Permits What He Could Prevent
71	The Attitude of the Pot
73	Serving From Love
75	The Perfect Note
77	The Word that Became Flesh!
79	Answering the Call
85	He Became Like Us!

Introduction

The world, being created and held together by Christ, must, then, by its very nature, preach Jesus.

Colossians 1:16-17, *For by Him all things were created, both in the heavens and on earth, visible and invisible, whether thrones or dominions or rulers or authorities—all things have been created through Him and for Him. He is before all things, and in Him all things hold together.*

I have found a witness to Him in everything from a butterfly to a human being. Traveling as I have in some one hundred fifty countries over two decades, I have also found Christ preached in some of the most intriguing folklore. It would seem that in every culture there are stories that, when heard, are recognized to be proclaiming truths about Jesus. I collect such stories and have put them in this volume for the readers' enjoyment and discernment. At first this was going to be a children's book, but I discovered that adults with childlike faith seemed to benefit the most from these tales. As you read, simply pray for a witness to the TRUTH that is within every believer.

The Stressed Vine

A man was touring some great vineyards and was amazed at the well-manicured vines. Some grapes were three or four times the size of any that he had ever seen. As he moved along examining the vineyard, he came upon a very pathetic-looking area, in which all vines appeared to be dying. He said to the guide, "Look at those vines that are nearly dead! The grapes are barely bigger than peas! The vinedresser should be dismissed." The guide smiled as he explained, "Those are called 'stressed grapes' and take more care than all the others. The vine must be held between life and death at all times, given neither too much water and fertilizer nor too little. Not too much pruning, but not too little, for these vines must be stressed. Because a vine thinks it is dying (but it will not die, for the gardener loves and cares for these vines more than any other), it will send its sweetness and life into the very small grapes, giving them 100 times the flavor and fragrance of the big grapes used to make the cheap wine. These stressed grapes are used to make the most expensive wine and will return a profit that is fifty, one hundred, or even two hundred times more."

We as God's children are the stressed grapes of the world.

Romans 8:17-18, *Now if we are children, then we are heirs also, heirs of God and co-heirs with Christ, if indeed we share in his sufferings in order that we may also share in his glory. I consider that our present sufferings are not worth comparing with the glory that will be revealed in us.*

Red-Faced Monkey

Colossians 3:2, *Set your mind on the things above, not on the things that are on earth.*

There is a story told in India about a magician who one day appeared in the village claiming to make gold. The man summoned everyone in the settlement and had the women bring him a large bowl of filtered water. As he began to stir the water with his walking stick, he plunged his other hand into his pocket and brought out a small bottle filled with black liquid, which he emptied into the bowl, and everyone watched as he continued stirring and the water turned black. At last he proclaimed, "I have made gold!" As the people looked up at him, with sleight of hand he let a few small pieces of gold fall into the water; he'd been hiding them in the hand that was holding the staff. Next he asked that the water be drained over a piece of fine linen. To everyone's surprise there was gold! A very rich moneychanger watched the whole event and approached the man with a request, "Is it possible for me to buy the formula that makes gold?" "Of course," the magician replied. "However, the cost will be 50,000 rupees!" The rich man was glad to pay the price, knowing how much money could be his by making gold. The magician wrote down the formula for the magical, gold-producing black liquid. The men made their exchange, and the moneychanger was departing quickly when the magician called, "Oh, there is something I forgot to tell you that you must never do. If you do it, the gold will not appear!" At that the moneychanger stopped, got out his pencil, and said, "What is it? I will write it down." The magician replied, "Put up your pencil. You will easily remember what I am about to tell you. When you are stirring the water and pouring in the black formula, and you see the water turn black, you must never, never, never think of a monkey with a red face! If you think of such a creature, the gold will not appear." The moneychanger ran off to make his fortune. However, every time he would see the water turn black from the formula, he would remember the warning not to think of the red-faced monkey, and in so doing he always thought of that monkey. In the end, there was never any gold. The man thought a change in location might help, so he tried making gold in the mountains, by the ocean, and in the jungle. It never worked, and finally he lost his mind, so vexed was he not to get the red-faced monkey out of his thoughts.

What gets the attention of Christians will get them. We will never be set free from the things on which we are focused. There are two ways to be controlled by sin. One is to constantly be thinking of participating in it, and the other is to constantly be consumed with staying away from it. Either way, sin is the focus. To be free, we set our minds on the things above.

Worms For Feathers

Romans 1:23, *and exchanged **the glory of the incorruptible** God for an image in the form of corruptible man and of birds and four-footed animals and crawling creatures.*

A gnome was pushing a wheelbarrow full of worms; he was a little man with a big nose, hands like shovels, and shoes like Arabian lamps. "Feathers for worms, worms for feathers," he cried as he walked. One little bird had been warned by his mother, "Be careful of the yellow cat; he loves to eat little birds." When the little bird met the gnome, he gladly exchanged one

little feather for a big, delicious worm. Day after day this went on, until one day the mother asked, "Why do you have a bald spot?" "Oh, I hit a tree flying," lied the youngster. Every day the exchange continued until one day, one feather too many had been traded. The cat appeared, the little bird could no longer fly, and you can guess the end. If we exchange the feathers, the truth of Jesus, for lies, we eventually lose our ability to fly. We are to mount up with wings as eagles, but those who would teach legalism slowly take our feathers and give us worms.

Jesus is the Way, and every other way is not the way. The world has its appeal, but only to the flesh of man. Christ's appeal is to the soul because of the happiness that He brings, for the purpose of obedience is to make the believer happy. Each morning I ask myself a simple question, "Mike, if you want to be happy, then follow Jesus. If you don't want to be happy, then choose your own way."

The Richest Man in the City

Matthew 6:19-21, *Do not store up for yourselves treasures on earth, where moth and rust destroy, and where thieves break in and steal. But store up for yourselves treasures in heaven, where neither moth nor rust destroys, and where thieves do not break in or steal; for where your treasure is, there your heart will be also.*

He was the wealthiest man in the city. One night, an angel appeared and spoke to him: "Tomorrow at midnight the richest man in this city will die." The rich man was vexed. He didn't sleep through the night, but planned his whole day. In the morning he set about putting his affairs in order. In the evening hours he sat and waited. It was 7:00 p.m., then 8:00 p.m., and so on. In fear he waited as the seconds counted down to midnight. At the twelfth strike of the clock, he closed his eyes, but later opened them to discover that he was still alive. The following morning he could hear wailing outside his window. Venturing out to the street, he heard the news: the baker had died at midnight. The entire population of the city was turning out to assemble at his home. All were recounting his acts of kindness, love, encouragement, and generosity. The rich man thought to himself, *I am only the richest man in the city in terms of material wealth, but that poor man was truly the one who was rich!* The problem with money is that it costs so much.

The Precious One Minute

It is said that a certain king of long ago ruled his area wisely and compassionately. He loved his family, the queen and their young son, and he passionately pursued hunting as a pastime, accompanied and assisted always by his companion, a large dog named Beth Galen. On one particular day, the king was not able to locate Beth Galen when he went off on a hunt, but he and his lords went anyway. Returning to the castle later in the day, he was horrified to meet Beth Galen in the hallway near the young prince's bedroom, for the dog had blood dripping from his face. Within seconds the king processed what had happened as evidenced by the sight before him; it was obvious to him that Beth Galen, who had always regarded somewhat jealously the jovial and affectionate relationship the king enjoyed with his son, had killed the youngster! Indignantly and spitefully the king withdrew the sword that hung at his side and with one swinging motion slew the large dog. Moving quickly into his son's bedroom to appraise the calamity, he found, as he had expected, blood splattered on the bed and walls, but as he tearfully took it in, he heard a whimper coming from behind the bed.

Rushing past the bed he saw what would conflict him with gratitude and guilt the rest of his life, for there, crouched in the corner, unharmed but pale, sat his son, fixated on a dead wolf lying before him. When the king saw that he had unjustly killed his own friend, who moments before had bravely saved his son's life, he went into mourning; it is said he never smiled again, and he decreed that the village be renamed "Beth Galen," the name it still holds today. The king could have waited one more minute before killing his good friend, but no, he believed he KNEW what had happened and lashed out.

How many times do we lash out at those we love the most among our friends and families? It may suit our flesh to cast aspersion elsewhere, but do they deserve it? Is our anger symptomatic of our own lack of understanding of situations, our own inability to find out the true facts, and our own selfish shortsightedness? The people who love us deserve the benefit of the doubt and our willingness to wait that precious moment to respect the love they have for us and to respond in kind. Romans 2:1, *Therefore you are without excuse, every man of you who passes judgment, for in that you judge another, you condemn yourself; for you who judge practice the same things.*

The Boxing Ring

There were two boys, one a boxer and the other a wrestler. They went to the same place for workouts. One day the wrestler noticed the boxer and invited him into the wrestling ring to fight. The boxer thought, *I am much bigger and will easily win*, and therefore agreed to the bout. However, once he entered the ring, the referee stopped him and made him remove his gloves and follow wrestling rules. There would be no boxing in the wrestling ring. The boxer was then beaten very soundly. A few weeks passed, and once again the wrestler invited the boxer to

fight. This time the boxer said, "You are very strong and beat me. Can you beat me in the boxing ring?" The wrestler, feeling confident because of the previous match, quickly gave his assent and entered the ring of the boxer, but was immediately stopped by the referee. "You must put on gloves, you may not wrestle, and you have to follow the boxing rules." The boy acquiesced, and though he was an expert at wrestling, he was no match for this boxer, who paid him back ten pains for each one pain he had initially levied on the boxer.

Every day we are surrounded by experts in the flesh. As believers, we are not conditioned to fight in the flesh. If we get in the ring with fleshly persons, we will lose. By listening to their insults and attempting to respond in kind, we will find ourselves defeated. But here is the secret: They have no training for our ring, the ring of the Spirit. Bless those who curse us, forgive, go the extra mile, compare ourselves unfavorably to Jesus, admit we have nothing, love, and walk in the Spirit, and we will heap burning coals on persons of the flesh.

A woman asked what to do when her husband was verbally abusing her. She was told to hug him and say, "I love you!" The woman returned at a later time to say, "When I started telling my husband that I loved him, he saw that he couldn't move me into a battle of the flesh, so he is now afraid of me and has run away." Previously, she had just gotten into his ring of the flesh and hurled abuses back at him, all without profit.

Philippians 3:3, *For it is we who are the circumcision, we who worship by the Spirit of God, who glory in Christ Jesus, and who put no confidence in the flesh.*

The Lost Key

Hosea 14:2, *Take words with you and return to the Lord.*

They tell a story in India of an evening when a man lost the key to his house. As the man was looking for his key under the streetlight, a neighbor came and inquired as to what the problem was. The man explained his dilemma, and at that the neighbor began to search with him. Soon another neighbor came, asking the same question and receiving the same response, and also began to help find the key. Soon over fifty neighbors were all looking for the key. In the end, one more neighbor came to ask what was happening. The man explained his situation again, but this neighbor asked a follow-up question, "Exactly where did you drop the key?" The man pointed up toward the house and said, "I lost it somewhere around the porch!" The neighbor wondered, "Why, then, are we looking all the way over here under the streetlight?" Frustrated at the interruption, the man who lost the key replied, "Can't you see that this is the only place where there is any light?"

How often we look for what we have lost in the place where it was not lost. In 2 Kings 6:5, the prophet lost his axhead in the river and cried out; Elisha explained that God would be happy to return it if the man would only point to the place where he had lost it. We lose the peace of God and the only place to find it is in the presence of God. We lose our victory and the only place to regain it is in His presence. In Him we will find everything.

The Lost Key

Hosea 14:2, *Take words with you and return to the Lord.*

They tell a story in India of an evening when a man lost the key to his house. As the man was looking for his key under the streetlight, a neighbor came and inquired as to what the problem was. The man explained his dilemma, and at that the neighbor began to search with him. Soon another neighbor came, asking the same question and receiving the same response, and also began to help find the key. Soon over fifty neighbors were all looking for the key. In the end, one more neighbor came to ask what was happening. The man explained his situation again, but this neighbor asked a follow-up question, "Exactly where did you drop the key?" The man pointed up toward the house and said, "I lost it somewhere around the porch!" The neighbor wondered, "Why, then, are we looking all the way over here under the streetlight?" Frustrated at the interruption, the man who lost the key replied, "Can't you see that this is the only place where there is any light?"

How often we look for what we have lost in the place where it was not lost. In 2 Kings 6:5, the prophet lost his axhead in the river and cried out; Elisha explained that God would be happy to return it if the man would only point to the place where he had lost it. We lose the peace of God and the only place to find it is in the presence of God. We lose our victory and the only place to regain it is in His presence. In Him we will find everything.

The Little Fish

Ask a room full of Christians, "If you want to be closer to Jesus, raise your hands!" Everyone who raises his hand is unbelieving, for we cannot get any closer to Jesus than to have Jesus dwelling in us. When we work for what we already have, we will lose what we already have, and a great deception in the Christian walk is to look for what is already ours. We don't need more, but we need the revelation of what we already have.

There is a story about a small fish that one day was talking with a big fish. The big fish asked, "What is the desire of your heart?" The little fish quickly responded, "Oh, one day I want to see the big ocean!" The knowledgeable larger fish asked, "Don't you know that you are in the big ocean?" The little fish looked puzzled, gazed around, and said, "Is this all it is?" To which the big fish responded, "By constantly looking for something else, you have been ignorant of what you have always had. Go and enjoy the big ocean." At that the little fish took off and made the discovery that his world had no boundaries.

2 Peter 1:3,4, *His divine power has given us everything we need for life and godliness through our knowledge of him who called us by his own glory and goodness. Through these he has given us his very great and precious promises, so that through them you may participate in the divine nature and escape the corruption in the world caused by evil desires.* For the Christian there is no such thing as a behavior problem; there are only belief problems. He has given us the very things for which so many continue to search. This awareness must come through revelation, and if we do not believe the things of God, He will see to it that our life has to prove them.

Rats!

Hebrews 12:2, *fixing our eyes on Jesus, the author and perfecter of faith, who for the joy set before Him endured the cross, despising the shame, and has sat down at the right hand of the throne of God.*

There is the story of a man who was testing a plane during World War II in Africa. In the airplane was a stick attached to the wing's control ropes. As the stick was pulled back, the ropes would tilt the back of the wings down, causing the plane to soar. As the stick was pushed forward, the wings would slant forward and cause a descent. When the pilot was in the air, he noticed that the stick was beginning to shake. His eyes followed the rope from the stick to the back of the seats, where he could clearly see the problem: There was a stowaway rat gnawing nervously at the control rope. The pilot thought to himself, "If

I turn my attention to the rat to chase it away, I will let go of the stick, go out of control and die. However, if I let the rat eat through the rope, I will also lose control and die." While pondering his quandary, the solution came to him. He simply pulled back on the stick, gave the engine full power, and gained altitude until the air became thin and cold. Soon the rat was frozen and released its grip on the man's future.

In life there are many rats; they can be in the form of our mates, our children, our circumstances, our health, or our finances. If we turn and face them, giving them our full attention, we will crash in despair. However, if we fix our eyes on Jesus and gain altitude, we will soon see that the rats drop off the control ropes of our lives. There is nothing that His nearness will not cure.

Money Isn't Everything

From Nepal we hear the story of a very clever man who was never seen doing anything, had few possessions, and was quite content. His friends were constantly accumulating more goods, but he, as stated, was content. Complaints eventually began to fill his wife's head, and she began to voice them, telling him he was lazy and lesser in stature than other men who had many acquisitions. He explained that men are not greater because of riches, and he would prove to her how easy it was to gain wealth. He went to a man selling candies at the side of the road and asked to purchase a handful. He then told the seller that he had to rush off to the cobbler's to pick up his shoes, and if the seller could come there to get paid for the candy, he would pay him double. The seller, in his greed, consented. Next the man went to the cobbler and asked for a new pair of shoes, telling the cobbler that he would be paid double by the seller of candy when he arrived. The cobbler went along with the plan, again out of greed. The man went on with new shoes and a handful of candy. When the seller appeared before the cobbler, both thought the other was there to make the payment. Upon discovering the truth of the matter, they set out on a journey to find the deceiver, who, in the meantime, had come upon a man doing laundry. The man gave him a piece of candy and showed him his new shoes, stating, "There are two men in the village that are giving away candies and new shoes. The laundryman said, "But I can't go, for I must guard the clothes while they dry." The man agreed to help by watching the clothes while the laundryman hurried off to get the free candy and shoes, but as soon as the laundryman was out of sight, the man took the clothes and left. The laundryman met the two men, discovered the trickery, and all three set out to find the man, who had stopped to hang the clothes on a tree to dry. As he waited, a herdsman passed with a bull, and the two men greeted one another. "Look at my tree!" said our bamboozler. "Clothes grow from it." The herdsman could see the profit to be made and asked if he could trade the bull for the tree. The man agreed but stipulated that he must be allowed to take the clothes that were this week's crop, and so off he went with the bull, the clothes, the shoes, and the candy. After a time the three searchers met the fourth man, who quickly joined them on their way to apprehend the crook. For the next ploy, the man put the candy in the bull's mouth, so when the bull walked, it would spit out the candy. A passerby, seeing a bull that could produce candy, offered many gold coins for the bull. Soon there were five men following the deceitful man. He dressed himself, entered the city, and went to the King's court to gamble. The King liked the man due to the image portrayed by the accumulated items and thought that he must be a very wealthy man. To gain his favor, the King gave him many gifts, and even called him "Brother." Just as he called him "Brother," the five men arrived ready to take the man, accuse him, and beat him. However, when they heard the word "Brother" and saw the man dressed so finely in the presence of the King, they said to one another, "This great man cannot be the man we are looking for," and they, too, were blinded by his image. They agreed to continue their search for the dispossessor, while the man returned home and gave his wife all of his newfound wealth. She praised him, but he only said, "The men of this place are full of greed and given to image.

It is quite simple to become rich in such a place. I am nothing special." He then returned to his lifestyle of contentment, having proven that the accumulation of wealth is not just for the gifted.

We live in a society where a man's worth is determined by his belongings. "What is the man worth?" means "How much money does he have?" To say "That man has millions" somehow implies that he has superhuman wisdom, talent, ability, and intellect. The Indians have a saying: "There are two ways to be wealthy. One is by the accumulation of wealth and the other is by the lowering of wants." Lower your wants and you will find yourself wealthy in nearly every situation. A friend with a ministry to lepers said, "Money isn't everything!" How true! The lepers had found Jesus and were content without hands or feet.

Luke 12:15, *And He said to them, "Beware, and be on your guard against every form of greed; for not even when one has an abundance does his life consist of his possessions."*

You Can't Put Water in a Full Cup!

Matthew 23:32, *Fill up, then, the measure of the guilt of your fathers.*

In India it is very important to have a Sadhu, a teacher. One day into the presence of a very famous teacher came a boy who was holding his cup of tea. The Sadhu was about to partake of his own pot of tea when the boy sat down, so he first took his pot and poured a full cup's capacity into the boy's already half-filled cup. The boy reacted as the hot liquid spilled over onto his legs and began to scream at the Sadhu, "You crazy old man, you are scalding me with your hot tea!" The old man looked at the boy and said, "Go away! You are in no need of me, for it is impossible to fill anything other than an empty cup! When you are empty, you may return."

God has a name, "I AM." I have a name, "I am not." He will be to me all that I am not, but He will not be to me what I am not until I admit what I am not. Once I admit that I cannot love, I can plug into His love. Once I admit that I am not holy, I can plug into His holiness. Don't lie in bed at night and think of all the things that you are not, unless you recognize that you are reciting your qualifications for usefulness. Power is perfected in weakness.

The Perfect Photo

A man had found the perfect woman, and on the perfect day, there was a perfect wedding. His friends were there to celebrate with him, and the friend he had known the longest was there to take the photographs, for the groom knew nothing of photography himself. After the wedding celebration, the young couple left for a honeymoon for a few weeks. Upon the man's return, he went straight to his old friend and requested the photos of the wedding. He said to his friend, "Let me see the

photos, for I remember how beautiful my wife was and how handsome I was." The friend reached into an envelope and handed the man the negatives of his wife. The man looked puzzled. "This is not my wife! I don't recognize her. She is white where she should be black and black where she should be white. This person looks ghastly. I would never marry anyone that looked like that. It is not she!" While he was so speaking, the friend's hand emerged from the envelope with another negative, this time of the groom. The man upon seeing it said, "This is not of me! I don't know the man! I was handsome on my wedding day. What kind of trick are you playing? Throw away all of the negatives." The friend laughed and said, "I am showing you the negatives, wherein are hidden the positive that you want, the image for which you are looking. Don't throw the negatives away." The man said, "How do I get the image as I remember it?" His friend replied, "It is very simple! Just follow me into the darkroom, and there you will find what you want." He said this not knowing how much the man was afraid of the dark. The man began to shake, "I don't like dark rooms." However, his friend persuaded him by saying, "You will never find the positive in the negative until you come into the dark." In that room the man watched with amazement as his friend developed the photos. In the tank of fluid the images began to emerge, and soon the man could see his beautiful wife and his own photo. In excitement he quickly grabbed both and started to leave, but his friend cautioned him, "The picture will only fade if you leave now. Let me dip it in acid, and the image will then be fixed." This he did, and the man left having found the positive that was hidden in the negative.

For the Christian there is a positive in every negative, but we must enter into the darkroom, the room of faith, in order to see it. In the darkroom everything we have looked to for support disappears. God's presence cannot be felt, there is no light, and the enemy constantly whispers, "If only you had done better, God would not have forsaken you." Finally, in that dark place the believer prays, "Father, if I walk in the valley of the shadow of death, I will fear no evil, for You are with me. I can't feel You, but You say You are with me, so You must be!" At that very moment the believer gives God something that no angel in heaven can: faith! Angels see Him and do not need faith, but in the dark when we cannot see and believe anyway, at that moment the light comes on and we see that He has never left us, and thus we see the positive—faith—that was in this negative experience. There are two types of faith people in chapter eleven of Hebrews, those who believe and receive and a greater group called the "others." The "others" are those who believed and never received, and yet they continued to believe. The world is not worthy of them, for the greatness of faith is measured not in how much one receives but in how long he can go and receive nothing. Oh, I nearly forgot; there is always a bath of acid in the darkroom that will fix the image of Christ in the believer, a baptism of fire that will stop the growth of the flesh life.

I John 3:2, *Dear friends, now we are children of God, and what we will be has not yet been made known. But we know that when he appears, we shall be like him, for we shall see him as he is.*

The Mysterious String

In India is told the story of a man who one night believed in Jesus and the next morning awoke to find a red string tied around his waist. The string was thin and as fine as silk, but it was unbreakable and, as he soon discovered, not removable. On most days the string was very loose and allowed the new believer to go wherever he wanted, but then on other days the string would pull him forward, taking him to destinations that he did not know. Some days he would resist the string, but it did no good, for the string would not let go. After several years the man noticed a correlation. When he sinned, the string would go loose, and then soon afterward, the string would go tight. Somehow this string was associated with his sin, but he didn't know how. Day after day the string would go loose and then tight, always pulling him forward until finally he found himself at the bottom of a large mountain. It appeared that the string was going to pull him to the top one day, and sure enough, by the next morning the journey had begun, and day by day he was inched toward the top. It was early one morning when he reached the summit of the mountain, and looking across the valley he could see the source of the string: it was Jesus! One end of the string was tied to the Father in Heaven and the other to the man. Every time the believer sinned, the string would immediately break, and almost as quickly Jesus would reach down, pull the two pieces together, and tie them, which resulted in the man's being pulled closer to the Father. The believer could see that in time he would be tied to the very presence of God. It was then that the revelation came to him that Jesus never let go of him and Jesus would bring him to the Father. Seeing the love of Jesus, the love of the Father, and the nearness of both, the man decided that he could no longer sin. Now that Jesus has died for our sins, He has earned every right to use sin. When a man is preaching with conviction about the love, mercy, forgiveness, goodness, and grace of God, that man is revealing his experiences. It is in our failures that we will find ourselves drawing nearer to Him, so we must never let the shame and guilt of failures drive us away. The Christian falls, but he always falls forward, on his knees and ever closer to the Father.

I John 1:9, *If we confess our sins, he is faithful and just and will forgive us our sins and purify us from all unrighteousness.*

The Great Meal in Heaven!

John 15:15, *No longer do I call you slaves, for the slave does not know what his master is doing; but I have called you friends, for all things that I have heard from My Father I have made known to you.*

In a vision a man was taken to the depths of hell, and what he saw there surprised him: Huge banquet tables were filled with every food imaginable, yet everyone seated around them was moaning, groaning, and gnashing his teeth. As the man approached he realized why. Though the tables were full of every food to delight both eye and palate, the people had no joints in their arms, which made it impossible to get the food to their mouths. The luscious food was always out of reach. Next the man was taken to heaven, where he saw the same beautiful banquet tables filled with every delight. This time, though, he heard shouts of joy and laughter coming from the great hall. He drew near and could see the difference. None of the residents of heaven had joints in their arms, either, but instead of complaining, they were feeding one another!

A man once exclaimed, "The problem with my family is that everyone is too selfish to think only about me!" There is only one thing that can truly feed selfishness, and, ironically, that is to be selfless. A selfless person is full, pressed down, shaken together, and running over with living water.

The Man in the Balcony

There was a very gifted pianist who was rewarded for his many years of study by being invited to play in one of the most famous concert halls in the world. His debut was greatly advertised. The result was a packed house; the social elite, the music aficionados, and representatives of the newspapers attended. The concert lived up to its billing and even wildly exceeded expectations. At the close of the concert, the pianist was surrounded by those wanting autographs, interviews, and

photos. An interviewer asked the pianist, "How does all of this attention feel?" The pianist responded, "I do not care about it; none of it matters, because I wasn't playing for any of these people." He pointed to the balcony where an old man was just getting up and leaving with the assistance of a walker. "See that old man up there? He was my first piano teacher; it was he who instilled a love of music in me. He knows more about music than I will ever know. I wasn't playing for any of you; I was playing for him, the man in the balcony. And while I was playing, I looked up and he smiled! That is why I am happy tonight, because he smiled at me." It is too nerve-racking and frustrating to try to please everyone. Only speak to the "man in the balcony," the Father above, who by His grace in us, through the presence of His Son, has put a love for Himself within us.

Colossians 3:17, *And whatever you do, whether in word or deed, do it all in the name of the Lord Jesus, giving thanks to God the Father through him.*

Your True Nature

Galatians 6:15, *For neither is circumcision anything, nor uncircumcision, but a new creation.*

In a village next to the Niger River I had noticed a cage holding one lone, odd-looking eagle. All the basic features were there; the body, neck, and two-thirds of the wings were white, yet the tips of the wings and the head were black. I was told, "That is a white eagle." Anyone could understand my confusion because of the black on its wings and the completely black head. I was then told, "It is a young white eagle; as the bird grows, the white will push its way to the tip of the wings and beak. The mature bird will be completely white." All things created are preaching Jesus. The DNA of the bird dictates that it will be a white bird. It grows into the revelation of what it really is in fact. It doesn't become a white eagle; it is a white eagle, even when the black is visible. Growth and maturity will force out what does not belong to the very nature of the bird. This is like the soul of man; the head is where the thoughts of the flesh hide in hopes of manifesting themselves. The black on the wings, our unbelief, is the only thing associating us with earthly living. Would it in any way be possible to stop the growth of this bird? No, but if it remained caged, the expression of its growth and maturity would never be seen. This white eagle gives me hope. First, it will grow, and what it is will be revealed; it has no choice. Second, God will not keep it captive. There will be a mounting up in the fullness of time. Imagine giving birth to a child if it were up to you to make it grow. Wouldn't you be a nervous wreck? You can't make a child grow, for that is God's work. Likewise, you don't make yourself grow spiritually! That is God's work, a work that He has ordained by writing into your very DNA that you are a child of God. In the end, you cannot make one hair [one feather] black or white. Your "color" is the outgrowth of the new nature that He has given you. Christ's life is written into your very nature. By the way, eagles devour the serpent and are feared by all the other little creatures that sneak about.

The proof of being a new creation is not revealed in one's victories but in one's struggles. As a new creation, a believer hates the things of the world in which at times he finds himself participating.

Being Content

A fisherman in Fiji had gone out in the morning, caught enough fish for the day, and returned to nap in a hammock attached between two coconut trees. He was soon awakened by a rebuke from a wealthy man. "What are you doing, sleeping like this in the middle of the morning? You own a boat, and you should continue to fish until sunset!" The fisherman earnestly asked, "Well, what would I do with the fish? I have enough already for my family!" The rich man replied, "You could sell them and get some money." "What would I do with the extra money?" asked the fisherman. "Well, you could buy more boats." Again, the fisherman inquired, "But what would I do with more boats?" "It is simple, man. With more boats you could hire more people and catch more fish and make more money!" Then the fisherman asked his final question, "But what would I do after I got all of that money?" Without thinking, the wealthy man replied, "Well, then you could afford to relax under a tree with no worries." The fisherman dismissed the wealthy man, saying, "This is what I am already doing!"

We cannot say that we have a God and live as though we do not have a God. The believer has the promise that he can be provided for as a sparrow and clothed like a flower, taking notice only of the concerns of today. We are not working so we can have rest, but we are given rest before we ever work. This kills the desire to find security in money. There are several purposes for money noted in the Bible, but none of them are security. We work, but not for security; we work as unto the Lord.

Colossians 3:17, *And whatever you do, whether in word or deed, do it all in the name of the Lord Jesus, giving thanks to God the Father through him.*

The Cracked Pot

2 Corinthians 12:9, *And He has said to me, "My grace is sufficient for you, for power is perfected in weakness." Most gladly, therefore, I will rather boast about my weaknesses, so that the power of Christ may dwell in me.*

A water bearer in India carried two large pots hung on each end of a pole borne across his neck as he walked the long distance from the stream to the master's house. One of the pots had a crack in it, and while the other pot was perfect and was always delivered with a full portion of water, the cracked pot arrived only half full.

Abiding Stories

Daily for two years this went on, with the bearer delivering only one-and-a-half pots of water to his master's house. Of course, the perfect pot was proud of its accomplishments.

But the poor cracked pot was ashamed of its own imperfection and miserable that it was able to accomplish only half of what it had been made to do. After two years of what it perceived to be bitter failure, it spoke one day by the stream to the water bearer. "I am ashamed of myself, and I want to apologize to you."
"Why?" asked the bearer. "Of what are you ashamed?"
"I have been able, for these past two years, to deliver only half my load, because this crack in my side causes water to leak out all the way back to your master's house. Because of my flaws, you have to do all of this work without getting the full value from your efforts," the pot said.

The water bearer felt sorry for the old cracked pot and compassionately said, "As we return to the master's house, I want you to notice the beautiful flowers along the path." Indeed, as they went up the hill, the old cracked pot took notice of the sun's warming the beautiful blossoms on the side of the path, and this brought it some cheer. But at the end of the trail, it still felt sorry that it had leaked out half its load, and so again the pot apologized to the bearer for its failure.

The bearer said to the pot, "Did you notice that there were flowers only on your side of the path, but not on the other pot's side? That's because I have always known about your flaw, and I turned it into great good. I planted flower seeds on your side of the path, and every day as we've walked back from the stream, you have watered them. For two years I have been able to pick beautiful flowers to decorate my master's table. Without your being just the way you are, he would not have such beauty gracing his home."

Will you pray that with each passing year you would become a weaker and weaker Christian? It is said that we are only as strong as our weakest link. This is not true for believers, who are actually only as weak as our strongest links. We never fail at our point of weakness but at the place where we think we are strong. Don't be ashamed of weakness. When God is dealing with us, He only requires weakness and emptiness.

Where to Find the Light?

On the island of Borneo there is the story of three boys and their mother. The mother wanted to hide the boys from the world and war so took them at a very young age deep into a mountain cave, where she made them a home. The boys were never allowed to leave the cave, for her fear was that they would be captured and forced to fight in a battle. In the cave they had all that they needed, even a library. When reading, the brothers could understand darkness, but they could not understand the references to daylight. Whenever the mother went to the village, she always admonished her sons not to leave the cave. However, after several years, on a certain day the boys did venture out. Approaching the entrance to the cave, they found the darkness that they knew too well, for it was already evening. Venturing further out, they became separated and lost. By daybreak, one boy found himself by a large tree, another was by the ocean, and the last was on a hilltop. As the sun rose they experienced daylight; the boys were captivated by the glory of the sun. Their minds flooded with the definitions of daylight and sun. In time they all found their way back to the cave, and meeting together, they began to share their wonderful experience of the sun. But soon an argument erupted, for one said the sun can only be experienced by a large tree, the other said it was by the ocean, and the last insisted that the sun could only be known on a mountain. Instead of rejoicing in each other's discovery, they separated and never spoke again.

In Luke 9:20, Peter gives the great confession that Jesus is the Christ, and then the rest of the chapter often deals with division. It is shown in brother against brother: "Who is the greatest among us?" It is shown through group against group: "They are not with us." It is portrayed in race against race: "Should we call down fire?" At Pentecost the Holy Spirit kills all such divisions, for the Holy Spirit was given to all believers, not just ministers, to every group, and to every race. If you believe that Jesus will meet you at the Baptist meeting, He will honor your faith. If you believe Jesus will meet you at the Pentecostal meeting, He will honor your faith. If you believe He will meet you at the tree, by the ocean, or on the mountain, He will honor your faith. We rejoice that others have found the Son, and we don't care who they are or where they were when they did so.

Romans 10:8-11, *But what does it say? The word is near you; it is in your mouth and in your heart, that is, the word of faith we are proclaiming: That if you confess with your mouth, "Jesus is Lord," and believe in your heart that God raised him from the dead, you will be saved. For it is with your heart that you believe and are justified, and it is with your mouth that you confess and are saved. As the Scripture says, "Anyone who trusts in him will never be put to shame."*

A Perfect Power

A young boy on a school trip was taken to the greatest waterfall in the world. He stood viewing it at the bottom, astonished by the power, the sound, and the shaking of the earth beneath him. Ever so gently, he removed a small jar from his school bag and unscrewed the lid. Next, he carefully stepped forward and caught some of the white foaming water in the jar, quickly replaced the lid, and returned the jar to his bag. That night during dinner his mother asked, "How did you like the waterfall?" The boy smiled, "I have a surprise for you!" He reached into the bag and with great care put the jar on the table. His hands were shaking excitedly as he unscrewed the lid. He knew what would happen: As soon as the lid came off there would be the very sound, power, and moving earth that he had experienced earlier. With one motion he removed the lid and quickly pushed the jar away. Nothing happened. The boy's countenance fell, and the mother asked, "What is wrong?" He replied, "I think that the water died."

Anything taken out of its source is dead, dead, dead. The commandments of Christ, taken away from the presence and infilling of Christ, are dead, dead, dead. Only one man ever lived the Christian life, and the only way that we will live it is if He lives it through us.

John 15:5, *I am the vine; you are the branches. If a man remains in me and I in him, he will bear much fruit; apart from me you can do nothing.*

Little Girl

Hebrews 12:2, *fixing our eyes on Jesus, the author and perfecter of faith, who for the joy set before Him* **endured the cross**, *despising the shame, and has sat down at the right hand of the throne of God.*

In Australia I heard the story of a little girl who was walking, skipping, and being very carefree on a beautiful Sunday. She first noticed the little bees working and commented, "Naughty, naughty bees! Grandpa would not like you working on Sunday!" Next she walked past a small group of birds singing and proclaimed, "Naughty, naughty birds! Grandpa would not like you singing on Sunday!" Finally, she passed a morose old donkey tied to a post and silently standing, doing no work. At this she

commented, "Poor, poor donkey! I feel so sorry for you! You have taken on Grandpa's religion!"

Where the burdens of worldly discipleship are advocated, there is no singing, but rather, distressful chants by spiritual patrolmen cautioning, "Do not handle, do not taste, do not touch!"

I am happy to be a Christian! To be Christian is to be in the most natural state a man can be. Every other religion is imposed on man, but Christianity is written into the very fiber of man.

How to Be Acceptable

Romans 14:17 & 18, *For the kingdom of God is not eating and drinking, but righteousness and peace and joy in the Holy Spirit. For he who in this way serves Christ is acceptable to God and approved by men.*

A wealthy man came with a very good question. He stood between two empty chairs and said, "In the chair on my right, I will put a man who is a Christian and is constantly telling others of Jesus and leaving bits of Scripture here and there. However, I know that the man is a secret alcoholic. In the chair on my left, I will put an atheist that doesn't drink and is very generous with the poor. Now tell me, how does the Christian who is an alcoholic go to heaven and the atheist that is a good man go to hell?" The man being asked the question said, "I have a question for you. You have a son that never works, has been married three times, and has stolen money from you. Is that true?" The rich man answered in the affirmative but wanted to know the point in the question. The other man replied, "I work hard, I am still married to the same woman, and I have never taken my father's money. Therefore, I am better than your son."

The rich man agreed but was still puzzled by the statement and said, "What does this have to do with my question?" The man responded, "Since you agree that I am better than your own son, I expect you to leave now, go to your lawyer, change your will, and leave everything you own to me." The rich man became angry, saying, "I wouldn't leave you anything!" "Why?" asked the poor man. "Because I don't care how good you are, you are not my son!" The poor man smiled, "Now you have answered your own question. I don't care how much better the atheist is than the believer, for the believer is born again as the child of God. Acceptance, just as for you, is not based on behavior but birth. I will take my stand with the child of God, and it does not matter if the atheist is good or bad, his fate is the same."

Is Christ acceptable to God? Is Christ near to God? Is Christ holy? Is Christ God's son? Is Christ your life? Then what is true about Jesus is true about your new life in Him!

Goat Priest

Luke 9:23, *If anyone wishes to come after Me, let him deny himself, and take up his cross daily, and follow Me.*

In a certain church in India, every priest wears a goatee. One young priest, it was discovered by his parishioners, had very boring sermons, and week after week he would watch the people yawn, sleep, and roll their eyes at his preaching. Then one Sunday morning as he began to preach, he looked over at an elderly woman who began to weep when his eyes met hers. He thought that after several years his preaching was finally touching the heart of at least one person. This encouraged him not only to continue preaching, but to add to the message, lengthening it every time he looked at the old woman, who was by now weeping louder and longer. At the conclusion of the service, the priest went running up to the old woman and said, "I noticed that my sermon touched your heart. What was I saying that made you weep so much?" She responded, "Actually, it wasn't your sermon. Last night my favorite goat died, and every time I looked at your mouth moving, your goatee would also move, and it reminded me of my dead goat!"

The Mogul King

I Corinthians 3:21-23, *So then let no one boast in men. For all things belong to you, whether Paul or Apollos or Cephas or the world or life or death or things present or things to come; all things belong to you, and you belong to Christ; and Christ belongs to God.*

In Him I will find everything that I looked for elsewhere in vain. There was a great Mogul King, a very different sort of king. He had been blessed by the loyalty and hard work of his people and was thinking how He might bless them. The king made the decision to take his most favored possessions and place them in the courtyard. He called all the people there and made a

Abiding Stories

proclamation. "Look around you and whatever catches your eye, go, put your arms around it, and it will be given to you!" The people were very surprised, for the king had placed in the courtyard carriages, vases, one hundred of his best horses, rugs, silver candlesticks, and more. Immediately they each began to put their arms around an object they wanted to take. The poorest boy in the kingdom stood watching the people and the king. Respectfully, fearfully, the boy approached the king with a question. "Is it true that whatever catches my eye in the courtyard can be mine?" The king answered, "Yes, it is true!" The boy hesitated and spoke again, "Do not be angry with me, but has Your Majesty thought about his offer?" The king said, "Look at the people and see for yourself. Whatever they see and desire in the courtyard is theirs once they put their arms around it. Go and do the same!" At that the boy stepped forward and wrapped his arms around the king's legs. The king was surprised and then smiled, "Now that you have me, all that I have is yours!"

I am convinced of this, that in Him we will find everything that we have looked for in other places in vain.

Choose the Easy Way Today and Prepare for the Harder Way Later!

Luke 9:62, *But Jesus said to him, "No one, after putting his hand to the plow and looking back, is fit for the kingdom of God."*

A friend from Brazil told me an interesting story from his youth. He had always wanted a dog without a tail. One day his father surprised him with a puppy, which quite delighted the boy, except that he noticed that the puppy had a tail. He finally said to his father, "I love the puppy, but I wanted a dog without a tail!" The father explained, "How do you think a puppy comes to have no tail?" Reaching into his pocket the man took out a pocketknife and handed it to his son. "Take this knife, go to the fence post behind the house, and cut the tail off." The boy, with dog and knife in hand, started off for the fence post. As he went along, the boy felt more and more his love for the puppy, and he thought, *I love the puppy, yet I want a dog with no tail. I know what I will do. I will only cut the tail off an inch at a time to avoid hurting the puppy so much at one time.* The boy did just as he thought and, in the end, had a puppy with no tail. However, the puppy would have much preferred that the tail had come off in one fell swoop.

Abiding Stories

The pain was only multiplied as the boy attempted to spare the puppy from it.

So often we choose the easy way today, thinking that we have avoided the difficult path. However, the difficult path will return and be much worse than if we had chosen it from the beginning.

The Vine and the Branch

A man was visiting the mountains from a different part of the country. While hiking, he discovered some of the wild grapes of the mountains and thought to himself, *I will cut a small shoot from this wild mountain vine and take it to my place for grafting.* After arriving back at his home, many miles away, he went to his neighbor, who owned a vineyard, and made his request. "May I graft this wild mountain branch to one of your native vines and watch it grow?" The neighbor said, "Of course you can, but you may not want to when you see what the grafting will entail." He explained the process as he pointed to a pile of cow dung. "At least once each day you must get cow dung with a bucket and mix water with it by hand until a thick paste is formed. Then you must take the mixture to the vine where the branch is grafted and pack the dung around the branch and vine. Thus will the branch be held in place until the vine can firmly take hold of it. The dung will also keep away diseases and bugs that hinder the branch from being grafted. If you love your little branch, you must learn to work in the dung!"

God is not fighting the fallen world but using it in our lives to keep us near to Him. It is in suffering that we will often draw near. He knew that in redeeming us and bringing us into the Son, He would have His hands in the dung. Those things that we consider to be our "thorns in the flesh" are the very things that have brought us near and kept us near.

II Corinthians 12:7-9, *To keep me from becoming conceited because of these surpassingly great revelations, there was given me a thorn in my flesh, a messenger of Satan, to torment me. Three times I pleaded with the Lord to take it away from me. But he said to me, "My grace is sufficient for you, for my power is made perfect in weakness."*

God Permits What He Could Prevent

Romans 8:28, *And we know that God causes all things to work together for good to those who love God, to those who are called according to His purpose.*

There is a true story that comes from Korea and has its beginnings in the work of a Bible distribution ministry. Korea was predominantly Buddhist for hundreds of years. A certain ministry acted on the assumption that women are more open to God than men and based its inception on giving small New Testaments to the young Korean girls as they left school. This is only half

of the story. A small boy was attending school when his father died. This caused him to quit school and begin to work to support himself and his mother. Next, his mother died, which left the boy a homeless orphan living under a bridge. Each day the boy would look for food. One day while in the fish market, the boy noticed that an old man was fumbling in his pocket for the money to pay for his freshly wrapped fish. The boy took the opportunity to steal the fish. As he ran through the market, fish under his arm, the men began to chase him yelling, "Thief, thief, thief!" The boy turned the corner and ran toward a small group of girls that had just received their New Testaments. One girl, feeling quite clever, held out her Bible and said, "If you want to steal something, steal this!" The boy obliged and grabbed the Bible as he ran past the girls. That night the boy enjoyed his ill-gotten fish and Bible. Each night he would read the Bible; once he'd reached the end of the book of John, he believed in Jesus. He could see from his place under the bridge the bright red neon crosses that were signs on churches. The boy decided to attend a church, and there he found companionship and love. Those at the church—knowing that he was an orphan and recognizing his heart for Jesus and his intelligence—made the choice to bring him in, provide for him, and continue his education. He finished school, Bible school, and seminary. In seminary he married, had children, and after graduation became pastor of a church that eventually numbered over 5,000 members. One Sunday he preached on how wrong it was for men to be keeping secrets from their spouses, because while this might have been a Buddhist custom (Korean men are typically very private), it was not Christian, for a Christian couple is one in Christ. In all the years of marriage the pastor had never confided in his wife the story of his youth and how he came to be a believer. He had kept the small Bible wrapped in paper, sealed with string, and hidden in a drawer. On this particular Sunday, upon arriving home, he was greeted by his wife, who was holding the small brown paper package and asserting, "You just preached that men are not to hide anything from their wives, and yet all these years you have hidden this package and refused to tell me what is in it. Today God has come for your words. What is in the package?" The man hesitated before saying, "I have kept this a secret because you have a very soft heart. I don't want to shame you, and you will cry when I tell you my story." At that his wife pressed all the more for an answer. He relented and told her the story of how his father died, then his mother, he was living on the street stealing his food, one day he stole a fish in the market, was chased, and happened past a group of young girls, one of whom held out her Bible and said to steal it, which he had done, then he'd read it, believed in Jesus, gone to a church, was taken in, sent to school, and that was how he came to meet her. Just as he expected, she began to cry, so he said, "You see? This is why I didn't tell you earlier. You are too soft. I knew I would shame you, and I knew you would cry." However, she replied, "That is not why I am crying. I am crying because I am the little girl that gave you that Bible!"

Doesn't God do everything exactly? Peter was in need of money. Of all the fish in the sea, Jesus sent the exact fish, to the exact hook, to the exact pole, to the exact man, to meet an exact need. Everything in our lives is exactly what we need. Everything passes through His hands before it reaches us.

The Attitude of the Pot

Gaze at Jesus and just glance at men and you will always be an optimist. Gaze at men and glance at Jesus and you will be a pessimist. Gaze at Jesus, glance at yourself and circumstances, and the peace that passes understanding will always be yours. Glance at Jesus, gaze at yourself and your circumstances, and you will surrender to decay.

There were two pots that were lowered each day into the deepest well in all of India, a well famous for its clear, cold, and refreshing water. One day one pot was being lowered as another was raised. As the owners paused, the pots met each other deep in the well. The pot ascending said, "I hate it down here; it is too deep and too dark. If it weren't for all the selfish people that like this water, I wouldn't have to keep coming here." The other pot was surprised and replied, "Yes, it is dark, deep and cold, but it is here that I find the thing desired by all men. The joy I receive from watching men drink in pleasure is greater than my discomfort! I am happy to find my value in descending into this dark place!"

Jesus may take you down to bring you up, put you out to bring you in, and give you a cross so that you might have a crown. Only in darkness do we find faith, and then we receive living water from which all men may drink.

II Corinthians 4:12, *So then, death is at work in us, but life is at work in you.*

Serving From Love

Deuteronomy 6:4 & 5, *Hear, O Israel! The LORD is our God, the LORD is one! You shall love the LORD your God with all your heart and with all your soul and with all your might.*

A man who had been the only child in his family told a personal story, though he was quite suicidal at the time he told it. It seems that his father and mother had loved and provided for him all of his life. His father was very proud of him, so the son often found himself the object of his praise. As the father grew old, it fell upon the son to be the caregiver, so he quit his job and spent the next six months caring for his father. All who knew of the son's dutiful devotion were overwhelmed by his loyalty and care, but as he related the story, he began to weep and explained his situation: "I only served my father for the inheritance. I knew he was dying and wanted to make sure that everything was given to me. I returned to my father's side only for gain. My father loved me, was proud of me, and always provided for me, and his reward in his last days was a son who cared more for the inheritance than for him. I have known many men who served their fathers while knowing that there would be no inheritance. They served out of love, but I out of greed."

So many are serving God only for the inheritance that will be theirs in heaven. If there were no inheritance, no heaven, no health, and no wealth, would that we served from love as a response to His greatness and faithfulness.

Job 13:15, *Though He slay me, I will hope in Him.*

The Perfect Note

John 12:32, *And I, if I am lifted up from the earth, will draw all men to Myself.*

In the Pacific Islands is a market wherein the mainstays of life are sold. At its entrance, an old man sits on a grass mat with his guitar. He can sing and play any song requested of him by the shoppers; many have tried to stump him, but it is nearly impossible. The interesting thing is that this man never moves his fingers on the guitar frets; he keeps his fingers in the exact same place for every song. An old man said to him, "How is it

that others who play the guitar move their fingers up and down the frets, while you never move your fingers and yet you play the song?" The man with the guitar answered, "It is quite simple! Everyone else is looking for the note that I found!"

I, too, have found the perfect note to play to others, and there is no need to move from it. I ask them to imagine that on one hand is Christ and on the other hand are problems. As they move the hand with Christ toward their eyes, they cannot see the problems; though those still exist, the people are not bothered by them. However, if they move the hand with the problems toward their eyes, they can no longer see Jesus and have no hope.

The Word that Became Flesh!

John 1:14, *And the Word became flesh, and dwelt among us, and we saw His glory, glory as of the only begotten from the Father, full of grace and truth.*

While visiting Korea I was taken to see a well-known painting. As I entered the room, I noticed a four-by-eight foot piece of canvas on which was written the complete New Testament in calligraphy (I was told that it was over 270,000 words). When my nose nearly touched the canvas, I could make out the tiny lettering and see that this was, indeed, the New Testament. The Koreans were very proud of the painting, but as for me, I didn't understand it. My mind was racing with the dilemma of what its purpose was. After all, who could carry this New Testament around? Why spend that kind of time copying such a thing? I figured the so-called artist must be obsessive-compulsive. Then the Koreans took me by the hand and made me back away from the canvas. As I did, something amazing began to be revealed. The artist, when writing each letter of the New Testament in calligraphy, had pressed either lightly or firmly with the ink in order to portray an image. As I reached the opposite side of the room, the image became quite clear: it was Jesus, with arms held out, and below Him was the caption, "And the Word became flesh and dwelt among us."

This is the distinctiveness of Christianity. All other religions are the word that became word, mere teachings without power. Christianity is the Word that became Flesh. Behind every word is His power in the promise or commandment, for the power and the Word are one in Him. Beautiful!

* Answering the Call

From India comes the tale of the time there was a very wealthy king, and as he approached old age, he knew he must deal with the fact that he had no heir. The counsel of his wisest advisors was that he should call together all of the young men from his kingdom and give each a task; the outcome of their efforts would help him choose his successor. So the king sent forth the proclamation that on a certain day, every young man was to report to the palace. The poorest boy in the kingdom, hearing the call, begged for his father's permission to go to the king. His father and uncles soundly rebuked him, saying, "You are the poorest boy from an unknown family; you are uneducated and have no talents a king would want." The boy agreed, but pleaded, "My state in life is not of concern; the greater concern is that my king has called me, and I must go to him, presenting myself as no better and no worse than I am." Seeing his determination, his father and uncles dismissed him, but laughed and said, "We will never see you again! The king will take offense at your lowly presence and will not welcome the likes of you."

* For an illustrated version of this story, the book *Sanji's Seed*, by B J Reinhard, is available.

On the long journey, the boy pondered what had been said to him and his own lowly state in life, but one thought compelled him, *If the king has called, who am I not to come? I will present myself just as I am, no better and no worse.*

Arriving near the castle, the boy's heart sank, for the road was completely lined with many well-dressed, talented, and educated boys. With the blare of a trumpet, the large wooden doors to the castle opened, and there stood the most magnificent man the boy had ever seen, his king. For a few moments he surveyed the glory of the king and wondered if he had made the right decision, but then his attention was captivated by what the king had to say. The monarch explained his dilemma; he had no son and must therefore pick his successor by way of assigning a task. Each boy was to step forward in turn, take one from a variety of seeds in a very large bowl, take the seed home with him, plant it, care for it, and nurture it for one year, at which time every boy would return to show the outcome. The boys expectantly lined up, each taking a seed from the larger-than-life pot. Their journeys home seemed shorter because of their hearts' fullness with expectation and hope. One thought lightened each step: *Could I be king?* Arriving home, the poor boy related the events of the trip to his relatives, who again discouraged him from dreaming that he could ever be a suitable king. The boy only responded that because his king had called him, it was his duty to go. The boy located a cracked pot and the best soil he could find in which to plant his seed.

In the coming year, despite the boy's constant care, it became evident that nothing was growing in the pot. The day of appraisal came; by now the boy had become accustomed to the mocking and jeering of his relatives. In disbelief they watched him—the poorest boy in the village with an old pot—depart to appear before the king. As he passed by them, he said only, "My king has called me, and I must go, no better and no worse than what I am." It was a long journey, for each footstep was weighted with dread of the king's scorn, rejection, and disapproval. Topping the hill his trepidation grew as he saw the many pots lining the road to the palace entrance. It was quite apparent that every boy had been successful with his endeavor, for emanating from those pots were fresh mangoes, coconuts, cashews, spices, and every other fruit, nut, and flower that delighted the eye. The boy took his place in the row and stood in the shade of the great plants with his pot of barren soil. The sharp and haughty ridicule hurled at him by the boys around him is not suitable to be recounted in this story. With the sound of the trumpet, the doors of the palace opened, and again the king emerged, adorned with much gold; his aide beside him carried the crown that was destined to belong to the boy soon to be identified as king. The ruler walked through the line and examined each boy's plant, tasting each nut and fruit. Upon reaching the poor boy's empty pot, the king looked, silently shook his head, and continued on to the next boy. After reaching the end of the road, the king turned back to reexamine each plant; again he stopped before the poor boy and his empty pot, but this time he spoke, "Why would you bring your king a pot with nothing in it?" In fear and embarrassment the boy answered, "You are my king! You called me, and I must come, presenting myself as no better and no worse than I am. I have failed you, but I thought it was more important that I obey than to have a fruitful plant." The boy had spoken without daring to look anywhere but at the ground, but since no word had come from the king, the boy stole a glance at his face, where he noticed a tear in the aged man's eye. The king gently smiled, grasped the crown, and said to the boy, "You shall be the next king! I killed the life within every one of these seeds by boiling them before I ever gave them out! Every boy here has deceived me with his phony results except for you. Because I called, you came, and you came in truth, no better or no worse. You will be my successor, the next king!" The crown was placed on the boy's head, a great reward for one who in simple integrity and honesty wanted to obey his king.

He Became Like Us!

Philippians 2:8 & 9, *Being found in appearance as a man, He humbled Himself by becoming obedient to the point of death, even death on a cross. For this reason also, God highly exalted Him.*

From the Amazon rainforest I was told an interesting story about a great chief who was traversing the forest when he happened upon a warrior much greater than himself. This warrior wore the scars of many battles. The chief noticed that his side, wrists, and feet had been speared. His face and back had also been wounded. The chief gave this great warrior the honor that was due him and sat with him, giving him his name. The warrior also gave his name, which was Jesus, and the chief was told that a white man would be coming to tell him more and he was not to harm the man but to listen. At that the warrior disappeared.

Jesus will meet a person where he is and in a way that He can be recognized. No one is forgotten by Him, and all are sought after by Him.